Deserts

PETER BENOIT

Children's Press®
An Imprint of Scholastic Inc.
New York Toronto London Auckland Sydney
Mexico City New Delhi Hong Kong
Danbury, Connecticut

Content Consultant
Donovan J. Craig
Research Assistant/Instructor
School of Environmental and Public Affairs
University of Nevada, Las Vegas

Library of Congress Cataloging-in-Publication Data

Benoit, Peter, 1955–
  Deserts/Peter Benoit.
       p. cm.—(A true book)
  Includes bibliographical references and index.
  ISBN-13: 978-0-531-20555-6 (lib. bdg.)   978-0-531-28104-8 (pbk.)
  ISBN-10: 0-531-20555-X (lib. bdg.)   0-531-28104-3 (pbk.)
  1. Desert ecology—Juvenile literature. 2. Deserts—Juvenile literature. I. Title. II. Series.
  QH541.5.D4B465 2011
  577.54—dc22   2010045962

All rights reserved. Published in 2011 by Children's Press, an imprint of Scholastic Inc.
Printed in China. 62
SCHOLASTIC, CHILDREN'S PRESS, A TRUE BOOK and associated logos are trademarks and/or registered trademarks of Scholastic Inc.

4 5 6 7 8 9 10 R 18 17 16 15 14 13 12

Find the Truth!

Everything you are about to read is true *except* for one of the sentences on this page.

Which one is **TRUE**?

T or F   It is always hot in the desert.

T or F   Antarctica is the world's largest desert.

Find the answers in this book.

Contents

THE **BIG** TRUTH!

The Desert Weather Report

The average scorpion is about 2.5 inches (6 centimeters) long.

4 Home, Sweet Desert Home

5 Wildlife Under the Sun

Clay brick house

Rocks, sand, and mountains are all common sights in the Atacama Desert.

CHAPTER 1

Exploring the Desert

If you take a trip to South America and stop by Chile's Atacama (ah-tuh-KAH-muh) Desert, don't bother packing an umbrella. You won't need a raincoat, either. Why? In the Atacama, less than 0.5 inches (1.3 cm) of rain falls each year. Some parts have not had rain in more than 400 years. This desert is sometimes called the driest place on Earth.

Some people of the Atacama region have never seen rain.

A sandstorm strikes the Sahara Desert. Saharan sandstorms can carry dust to Greenland!

CHAPTER 2

With Sand and Wind

How do deserts form? It depends on the type of desert. One kind is formed when moist air near the **equator** rises, eventually forming precipitation. After losing its moisture, the air moves north or south. It sinks and warms up. This hot air settles in or blows across regions where deserts are found. There is very little **humidity** in the hot air. This is how deserts such as the Sahara formed.

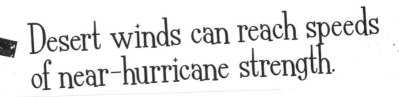

Desert winds can reach speeds of near-hurricane strength.

Other Types of Deserts

Some deserts are called rain shadow deserts. They form near mountains. The mountains block rain from reaching the land past them. Only dry air reaches the other side. This is how the Gobi Desert in China was created. Another type of desert is found in very cold areas. Temperatures are so low the air cannot hold much water. Such deserts are found in Antarctica and Greenland.

One-fifth of the world's land surface is desert.

A group of scientists travel through the Gobi Desert. Many dinosaur remains have been found in the Gobi.

Mountains of Sand

Sand dunes look like mountains but are able to move and drift with enough wind. A dune is usually created by wind blowing in one direction. Grains of sand are pushed into a large pile. Dunes can grow to amazing sizes. Some are miles long and hundreds of feet tall! They form in a number of different shapes, and no two dunes are exactly alike.

Long stretches of dunes are called *seifs*. Curved dunes are *barchans*.

In ancient times, this oasis was the site of a lake.

Finding an Oasis

An **oasis** is an area of a desert with a source of freshwater. This water often comes from under the ground. These freshwater springs allow some plants and trees to grow. In turn, they provide shade from the sun and heat. Sometimes, crops such as lemons are grown in oases.

The Kharga Oasis

In some deserts, communities and towns have formed around oasis areas. The Kharga Oasis in the Sahara is one of the biggest in the world. It is more than 100 miles (161 km) long. More than 60,000 people live around it. Some of them specialize in making baskets and mats out of the leaves of the palm trees growing there.

Every part of a palm tree is used by people living in the desert.

There are more than 2,500 species of palm trees.

17

The Desert Weather Report

Deserts are harsh places. The weather is extreme. When it is hot, it is very hot. Heat waves ripple up from the baked ground. When it is cold, it is very cold. The sun sets and the temperature drops fast. When the wind blows, it blows hard. Sandstorms fill the air with grainy bits. When it rains, it pours. A sudden cloudburst can release several inches of rain in a single hour!

Summer thunderstorms are common in some deserts.

Hot and Cold

Some deserts are very hot during the day. Highs can pass 100°F (37.8°C). But in cooler months, temperatures can dip below freezing at night.

Polar Deserts

In most of Antarctica, the temperature stays below freezing all the time. Winds sometimes blow more than 100 miles (161 km) per hour. Brrr!

A wadi is a gorge cut by rainwater in the desert. Most are dry, but they can fill up in a flash flood.

CHAPTER 3

Man-made Deserts

Most deserts were created by nature over thousands of years. Humans, however, are responsible for making many deserts grow much larger. In fact, deserts all over the world are growing every year. This process is known as **desertification** (deh-zur-tih-fih-KAY-shuhn). Desertification causes problems. It becomes harder to grow crops or raise animals on desertified land. Drinkable water becomes scarce.

 Wadis are also known as washes, coulees, and arroyos.

Recipe for a Desert

In many areas near the edges of deserts, people cut down trees to use as firewood. They need the firewood for cooking and keeping warm. The cutting down of trees is called **deforestation**. Also, people have herds of animals, such as goats and sheep. These animals eat any grass growing in the area. Overgrazing is when animals eat grasses in fields to the point of damaging the plants. The ground becomes bare and cannot hold water. Wind blows the soil away. The land becomes a desert.

People living near China's Tengger and Badain Jaran deserts must fight against desertification.

22

Desert homes are often painted white to help them stay cool.

Small windows help keep sand out of houses in the desert.

Water and Desertification

Another factor that can lead to desertification is **irrigation** (ihr-uh-GAY-shuhn). An area can become a desert when its water supply is pumped away. Water can be redirected from a natural source to water crops. Water can also be redirected to supply drinking water to communities. Sometimes the water contains salt. Salt builds up in the land being supplied with the water. Eventually, the land cannot support plant growth.

Overgrazing has contributed to desertification in parts of Australia.

Two-thirds of Australia is made up of deserts and semideserts.

Stopping the Spread

How can the spread of deserts be stopped? Experts are looking at many possible answers. Some people plant trees and bushes at the edge of deserts. This helps stop the wind from blowing away the soil. In the Tengger Desert in China, people put straw fences in the ground. This also helps stop the sand from spreading.

Other Ideas

What else can be done to help stop the growth of deserts? One idea is **afforestation** (a-for-eh-STAY-shuhn). This involves planting trees and grasses in key areas around the borders of deserts. Putting a fence around the new growth so that animals cannot get to it is also helpful. Teaching people about how to use water supplies—and how not to—is important, too.

Plant roots help anchor soil. Planting trees and shrubs helps reduce the amount of soil blown away by wind.

Bedouin tents are easily transported to new locations.

CHAPTER 4

Home, Sweet Desert Home

Roughly 1 billion people on this planet call the desert their home. These people have found ways to survive in areas that have little water and extreme temperatures. They know where to find and grow food. They've learned what it takes to survive in some of the world's harshest places.

 The Bedouin of the Sahara call themselves "people of the tent."

Desert Dress

Different desert peoples wear different kinds of clothing. Some wear modern clothes. Many wear more traditional clothing. This includes long-sleeve, full-length robes of loose, white fabric. The loose material allows breezes to cool the skin. The robes cover all but the hands and head. They protect the skin from the harsh sun. Some groups wrap long cloths around their heads and faces for protection from the sun.

Bedouin head coverings are usually made of cotton and come in a variety of colors and patterns.

Desert people must keep cool and protect themselves from the sun at the same time.

28

Some desert homes are tall and narrow, with areas of shade between them to help keep people cool.

Keeping Cool

The homes of desert people vary from place to place. In some areas, homes are built with thick walls. These walls absorb the sun's heat, helping it stay cool inside. During chilly nights, the warmed walls give off some of this heat. They help keep the interior from becoming too cool.

Nomads at Home

Some people in the desert move from one place to another with their flocks of sheep or goats. They keep shifting in search of water and food. These people are often called **nomads**. Some live in tents made of fabric. Others build huts out of clay or straw. Some groups leave the huts behind when they move on.

Camels are the main source of transportation for many desert people.

Some nomads take shelter in simple cloth tents.

Gobi houses often have a hole at the top to let out smoke from cooking.

A Tent Home

Many groups of people who move through the desert bring their homes with them. The people of the Gobi Desert, for example, live in a type of tent. A wooden framework is covered with a type of cloth called felt. The felt is made from sheep's wool. The structure can be rolled up and taken along with its traveling owners.

Clay bricks help protect against extreme desert temperatures.

Sun-Dried Brick

In the Sahara Desert, many homes are made out of bricks. People mix water with clay and dirt. The mixture is placed in a mold and allowed to dry in the sun. When the bricks are ready, they are used to build walls. More clay is used to paste the bricks into place.

A Bundle of Sticks

In the Kalahari Desert in southern Africa, traditional homes of the San people are very simple. These shelters are often made of branches and dried grasses. When the people move on to another place, they give the house back to nature.

The San people of southern Africa live together in bands made up of several families.

Homes of straw and grass do not protect against the weather as well as clay homes do.

Desert tortoises can be found throughout the Mojave Desert.

CHAPTER 5

Wildlife Under the Sun

Do you think of deserts as lifeless places? Think again! Just as people have found ways to survive in the desert, so have many kinds of plants, insects, and animals. In fact, a number of fascinating species can be found in deserts around the world. Each has adapted to life where the weather is extreme and water is scarce.

Fully-grown desert tortoises weigh between 8 and 15 pounds (4 and 7 kilograms).

Plants

Most desert plants grow far apart so they do not have to share what little water there is. Some plants, such as cacti, have shallow roots that spread out under the ground. This allows the roots to soak up water as fast as possible during those rare rainstorms.

Shallow cactus roots

Timeline: Oil in the Desert

1930s
Oil is discovered in the Arabian Desert.

1950s
World demand for oil explodes as more people begin driving cars.

From Plants to Petroleum?

Petroleum, or oil, is used to make gasoline and other products. Some of the world's most important oil supplies are found in deserts. These supplies have made certain desert nations wealthy. Many scientists believe that petroleum formed from the remains of marine plants and animals. Through extreme heat and pressure, the remains became petroleum. These changes took millions of years. Oil is usually deep underground and is reached by drilling.

2008

Saudi Arabia is the world's top oil producer.

2002

Middle Eastern desert countries produce roughly one-fourth of the world's oil.

The Saguaro cactus is found only in parts of Arizona and Mexico.

The Hardy Cactus

Some of the most amazing desert plants are cacti. They can store water in their stems. The saguaro cactus can soak up as much as 1 ton of water during a big storm. Its skin stretches to allow it to expand. The saguaro also grows very slowly. After 30 years, it may only be a few feet tall. Eighty years later, it will still be growing.

Waiting for Rain

A number of flowers and plants in the desert start out as seeds that are just waiting for rain. They lie in the ground, often for years, until rain begins to fall. Then, they spring into action. They sprout very fast. They grow, bloom, produce new seeds, and then die in a short time. After a heavy rain, the desert is a stunning sight full of color and beauty.

Although they do not live long, desert flowers are beautiful.

Death Valley is the hottest and driest place in North America.

Creepy Crawlies

Arachnids (uh-RAK-nidz), including spiders and scorpions, live in the desert and survive by getting water from the prey they capture. In some deserts, the trap-door spider hides in a burrow with a hidden door. When a tasty snack stops nearby, the spider jumps out, grabs it, and drags it below. In other deserts, tarantulas nearly as large as a person's hand track down lizards, insects, and other prey.

Arachnids, such as this scorpion, have hard outer skeletons.

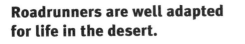

Roadrunners are well adapted for life in the desert.

Roadrunners swallow their prey headfirst.

Other Desert Dwellers

How do other creatures survive in the desert? Many get water from what they eat. The roadrunner gets its water from the bodies of small snakes and lizards. Lizards get water from insects. In the Kalahari and Namib deserts, the gemsbok, a type of antelope, gets water by eating a melon called a *tsamma*. Other animals, such as the desert tortoise, can store extra water.

More Survival Skills

Some animals survive in the desert by sleeping during the heat of the day. They are **nocturnal**, active at night when it is cooler. Some have light-colored fur, which soaks up less heat. Other creatures, such as certain foxes, have very large ears. These ears help release body heat.

A desert is extreme. It is also quite beautiful. Perhaps most importantly, for many plants, animals, and people, it's home. ★

Some desert foxes weigh less than pet cats.

Desert foxes dig burrows in the sand to help stay cool.

True Statistics

Largest desert in the world: Antarctica, at 5.4 million sq. mi. (13.9 million sq km)

The highest temperature recorded in a desert: 136°F (57.8°C) in the Sahara in 1922

Amount of Earth's surface covered by deserts: 20 percent

Average rainfall per year in a desert: Less than 10 in. (25 cm)

Driest desert in the world: Atacama Desert in South America

Average rainfall per year in the world's driest desert: Less than 0.5 in. (1.3 cm)

Number of people who live in the world's deserts: Approximately 1 billion

Tallest of all cactus plants: Saguaro cactus, reaching heights of up to 50 ft. (15 m)

Amount of Sahara Desert covered by sand: 20 percent

Beavertail cactus

Did you find the truth?

(F) It is always hot in the desert.

(T) Antarctica is the world's largest desert.

43

Resources

Books

Barnes, Julia. *101 Facts About Deserts*. Milwaukee: Gareth Stevens Publishing, 2004.

Dayton, Connor. *Desert Animals*. New York: PowerKids Press, 2009.

Green, Jen. *Deserts and Polar Regions Around the World*. New York: PowerKids Press, 2009.

Greenberger, Robert. *Deserts: The Living Landscape*. New York: Rosen Publishing Group, 2009.

Jackson, Kay. *Explore the Desert*. Mankato, MN: Capstone Press, 2007.

Legg, Gerald. *Life in the Desert*. New York: Children's Press, 2005.

Lundgren, Julie K. *Desert Dinners: Studying Food Webs in the Desert*. Vero Beach, FL: Rourke Publishing, 2009.

Phillips, Dee. *Find It in the Desert*. Milwaukee: Gareth Stevens Publishing, 2006.

Wojahn, Rebecca Hogue, and Donald Wojahn. *A Desert Food Chain: A Who-Eats-What Adventure in North America*. Minneapolis: Lerner Publications, 2009.

Organizations and Web Sites

National Geographic: Deserts

http://environment.nationalgeographic.com/environment/
habitats/desert-profile/

Read more about deserts and how creatures survive in them.

National Geographic Explorer!: Featured Quick Flick

http://magma.nationalgeographic.com/ngexplorer/0403/
quickflicks/

Watch a short video clip to learn more about desert ecosystems.

The Nature Conservancy

www.nature.org/

This site will connect you to more than three dozen links to
desert information.

Places to Visit

Arizona-Sonora Desert Museum

2021 North Kinney Road
Tucson, AZ 85743
(520) 883-1380
www.desertmuseum.org/
Explore a botanical garden,
natural history museum, and
zoo to learn about the region.

Desert Discovery Center

831 Barstow Road
Barstow, CA 92311
(760) 252-6060
www.discoverytrails.org/
welcome1.html
Learn more about the Mojave
Desert at this interactive
learning center.

Important Words

afforestation (a-for-eh-STAY-shuhn)—the process of turning land into a forest by planting trees

arachnids (uh-RAK-nidz)—creatures, such as spiders, with four pairs of legs

deforestation (dee-for-eh-STAY-shuhn)—the clearing of forests or regions of trees

desertification (deh-zur-tih-fih-KAY-shuhn)—process in which land becomes drier and drier until it cannot support plant life

equator (i-KWAY-tur)—an imaginary line around the middle of Earth

evaporation (i-vap-uh-RAY-shuhn)—the process in which a liquid becomes a gas

humidity (hyoo-MIH-dih-tee)—the amount of moisture in the air

irrigation (ihr-uh-GAY-shuhn)—the supplying of water to an area through man-made methods

nocturnal (nok-TUR-nuhl)—active at night

nomads (NOH-madz)—people who move from place to place as needed to find enough food and water

oasis (oh-AY-sis)—an area of a desert with a source of freshwater

precipitation (pri-sip-i-TAY-shuhn)—the falling of water from the sky as rain, snow, sleet, or hail

Index

Page numbers in **bold** indicate illustrations

About the Author

Peter Benoit is educated as a mathematician but has many other interests. He has taught and tutored high school and college students for many years, mostly in math and science. He also runs summer workshops for writers and students of literature. Mr. Benoit has also written more than 2,000 poems. His life has been one committed to learning. He lives in Greenwich, New York.